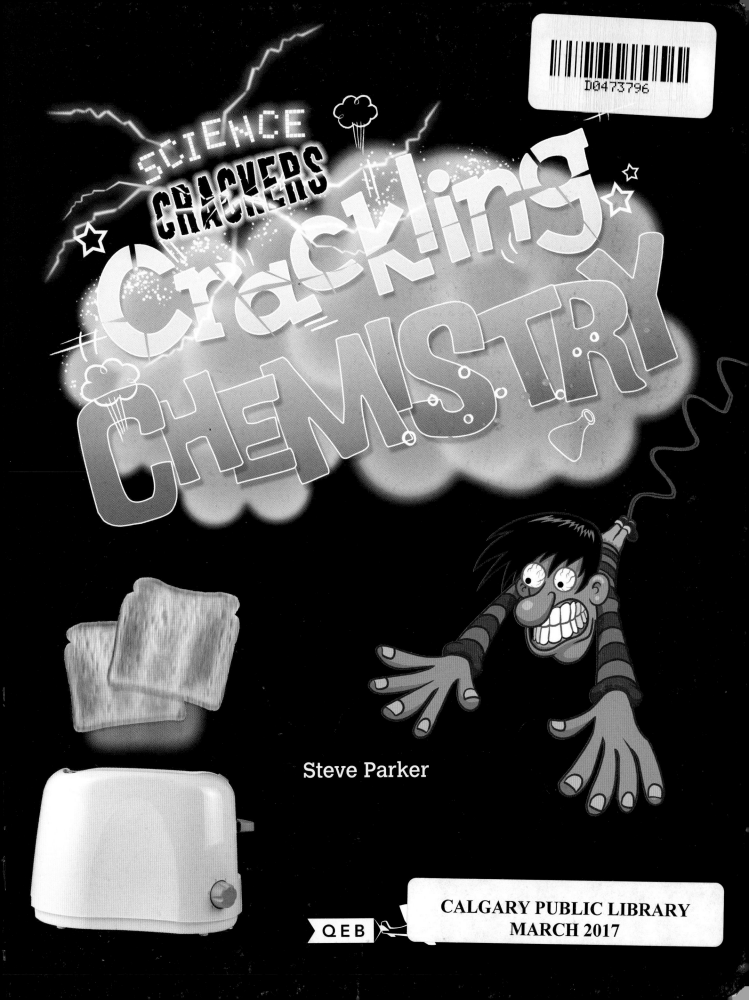

SCIENCE CRACKERS

Crackling CHEMISTRY

Steve Parker

QEB

Quarto is the authority on a wide range of topics.
Quarto educates, entertains and enriches the lives of
our readers—enthusiasts and lovers of hands-on living.
www.quartoknows.com

Created for QEB Publishing, Inc. by Tall Tree Ltd
www.talltreebooks.co.uk
Editors: Rob Colson and Jennifer Sanderson
Designers: Jonathan Vipond and Malcolm Parchment
Illustrations, activities: Lauren Taylor
Illustrations, cartoons: Bill Greenhead

First published in hardback in the United States in 2011
by QEB Publishing, Inc.
Part of The Quarto Group
6 Orchard, Lake Forest, CA 92630

A CIP record for this book is available from the Library of Congress.

ISBN 978 1 68297 0 263

Printed in China

Picture credits
(t=top, b=bottom, l=left, r=right, c=center)
Alamy: 13b Arco Images GmbH, 18 Chris Howes/Wild Places Photography, 27b Justin Kase zninez;
iStockphoto: 17tl; **NASA:** 23b; **Science Photo Library:** 2 and 20b George Chan, 21bCharles D Winter,
27t Tek Image; **Shutterstock**: 1 and 29t Aleksandr Stennikov, 4 Nanostock, 5b Kamira, 6l Burhan Bunardi
Xie, 6r Stuart Monk, 7cl Sebastian Crcoker, 7cl Jiri Hera, 7cr vnlit, 7bl stefanolunardi, 7br Iwona Grodzka,
8bl Eric Isselée, 9tl Claudio Bertoloni, 9lct Pakhnyushcha, 9lcb Melinda Fawver, 9bl Zagibalov Aleksandr,
9tr Stephen Aaron Rees, 9br Eric Isselée, 11 br Mushakesa, 12tl Roman Chernikov, 12bl iofoto, 12br
Kiselev Andrey Valerevich, 13t Eric Gevaert, 17bl Elnur, 16 AdamEdwards, 17r Steve Lovegrove, 20 Boyan
Dimitrov, 21c DGDESIGN, 22t Evgeny Boxer, 22b OtnaYdur, 23c LoopAll, 26t Andrew Kendall, 26c
Photoroller, 27c IIFede, 28t nito, 28b AVAVA, 29b Filipe B. Varela; **Wikimedia Commons** 7t,

Note
Web site information is correct at time of going to press. However, the publishers
cannot accept liability for any information or links found on Internet web sites,
including third-party sites.

In preparation of this book, all due care has been exercised with regard to the activities and advice
depicted. The publishers regret that they can
accept no liability for any loss or injury
sustained.

The practical activities in this book have been
checked for health and safety by CLEAPPS, a
UK-based organization that provides practical
support and advice on health and safety in
science and technology.

Words in **bold** are explained
in the Glossary on page 31.

CONTENTS

NOT MUCH USE!

What are these pages made of? Paper, of course. Paper is thin, light, **flexible**, and good for printing words and pictures. Paper is the right material, or substance, for the job. Imagine if these pages were made of bricks!

There are hundreds of different materials and substances all around you. Each one is designed for a certain use or task, and has certain features. It can be hard or soft, stiff or flexible, smooth or rough, and light or heavy. Materials are chosen for their different combinations of features.

IMAGINE THIS...

Some of the hardest materials are metals, such as iron and steel. They make sharp blades harder than the things they cut. A chocolate knife would be no good! Some metals are so hard they can be cut only with a powerful flame.

WHAT ABOUT ME?

Which materials do you use every day? Clothes are made from soft and warm fabric. Umbrellas need to stop the rain. They would not be any use if they were made from paper!

OOOPS!

Sponges are very good for washing in the bathtub. They are soft and springy and full of holes that fill with soapy water. But because they are so soft and springy, they are no good for building houses!

SHAPING

Statues and carvings are made from materials we can cut, shape, and polish easily, such as wood and stone. They can be cut and shaped using metal tools. Imagine carving a statue out of floppy jello!

GOOD AND BAD

Glass is good for windows. It lets light through so we can see what is on the other side. But glass has a problem, too. It is fragile and can break into very sharp pieces. We know we must be careful with it. The benefit of glass being seethrough is bigger than the problem of it breaking.

NATURAL OR NOT?

Can you make diamonds in an oven? Do plastic toys grow on trees? Some materials and substances are natural, or found in nature. Others are **artificial** and made by humans.

Substances that come from nature include many kinds of wood and stone, which we use for making furniture and houses. Artificial substances include plastics, some metals, glass, and pottery. They are produced from natural materials. We change these natural **raw materials** to make them hard, tough, and longlasting.

STRONGER THAN NATURE

Skyscrapers could not be built from natural materials alone. Stone is too heavy and wood is too weak. We need to use an artificial metal called steel to make the strong girders.

USEFUL FOR BUILDING

People have used wood and stone for building for thousands of years. Wood may rot and weaken, but stone can last forever. The Great Sphinx and pyramids of Ancient Egypt were built from stone around 4,500 years ago.

PRECIOUS MATERIALS

Precious gems and jewels such as diamonds and rubies are natural. They are found in rocks and then smoothed and polished so they sparkle. Other precious natural materials include metals, such as gold and silver.

BACK TO NATURE

Many natural materials can be **recycled** by nature, but most artificial materials cannot. We must recycle them ourselves. You can recycle glass, some plastics, paper, and cans by sorting them and taking them to a recycling center.

IMAGINE THIS...
See how much of your everyday waste you can recycle—you might be surprised by how much garbage you can save.

Aluminum and steel cans

Newspapers, magazines, and cardboard packaging

Plastic bottles

Glass bottles

HARD AND SOFT

Soft, flexible materials are no use for building houses or bridges. And hard materials are useless for making clothes or sheets for your bed.

We make clothing, bedding, and similar products from natural materials such as cotton and wool. These contain millions of tiny, bendy, threadlike fibers that are woven or knitted together to create soft, bendable materials. Many kinds of metals are quite stiff or **rigid**, but they are also slightly flexible. They can bend a little rather than break.

NOT TOO LONG

Soft substances such as sponges and foams are made from elastic materials that bend and then spring back to their original shape. Bungee jump cords are made from very strong elastic material, such as tough rubber. The amount of stretch must be checked and measured often, to make sure they are safe and not weak or worn.

SHARK ATTACK?

Water is very heavy and it can push with great force. Big tanks or aquariums have glass sides that are extra-thick, so they do not crack under the pressure.

HARD

Diamond

Knife blade

Hardness is determined by how well an object scratches something. Harder objects scratch others more easily.

Copper coins

Pencil lead

SOFT

HANDLE WITH CARE

Some materials are very rigid—if you bend them too much, they will break. We say they are **brittle**. Glass and pottery will crack and snap into sharp pieces that are dangerous.

WOOL FOR US

Wool for fabrics is the long, soft hair or fur from sheep and other animals. About once each year, the wool is cut off or sheared, then it grows again. It doesn't hurt—it's like when you get a haircut.

STRONG AS... PAPER?

Different materials are suited to certain tasks. For example, paper is flexible and floppy. Or is it? The shape of an object can be as important as the material from which it is made. The challenge is to rest a book on top of upright sheets of paper.

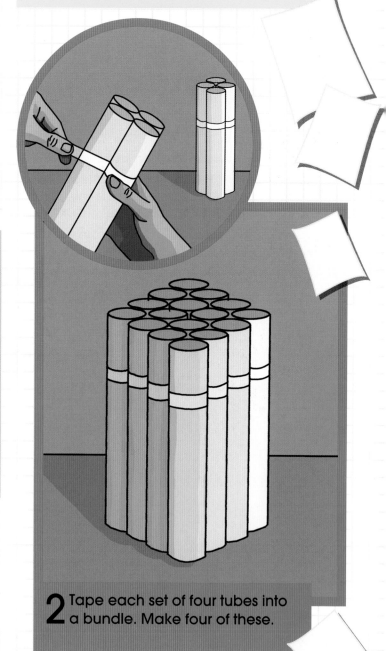

1 Try to stand the paper sheets on their ends. They cannot hold themselves up, let alone support a book. Roll each sheet of paper into a tube shape about 1¼ inches across and tape the ends together firmly.

2 Tape each set of four tubes into a bundle. Make four of these.

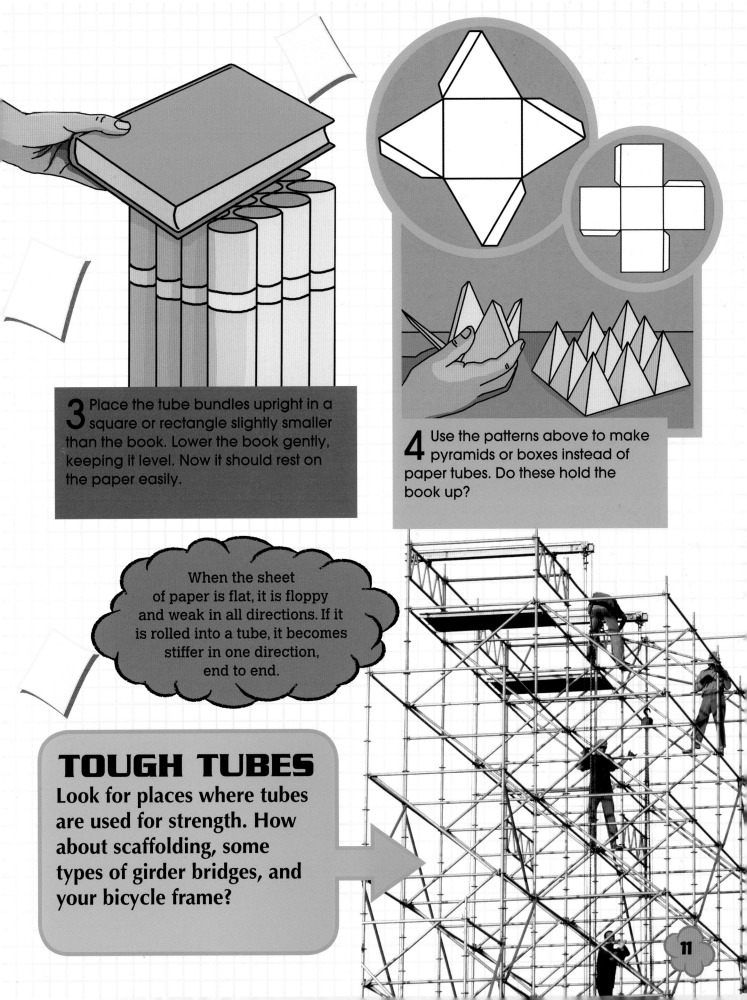

3 Place the tube bundles upright in a square or rectangle slightly smaller than the book. Lower the book gently, keeping it level. Now it should rest on the paper easily.

4 Use the patterns above to make pyramids or boxes instead of paper tubes. Do these hold the book up?

When the sheet of paper is flat, it is floppy and weak in all directions. If it is rolled into a tube, it becomes stiffer in one direction, end to end.

TOUGH TUBES

Look for places where tubes are used for strength. How about scaffolding, some types of girder bridges, and your bicycle frame?

ALL MIXED UP

Substances can get mixed up. Sometimes you can separate them, but other times substances seem to disappear—like sugar stirred into hot water. Where has the sugar gone?

A mixture is two or more substances blended together, which can be separated easily. But when sugar is added to water, it breaks up into pieces that are much too tiny to see. They spread out and float around in the water. This is called **dissolving**. A substance that dissolves is called the **solute**. What it dissolves in, for example water, is the **solvent**. Both together are the solution. There are other types of mixtures, such as suspensions and emulsions.

MIX IT UP

A suspension is a type of mixture where a solid substance is mixed with a liquid, usually by shaking or stirring them together. An emulsion is a special kind of mixture made up of two liquids that do not normally want to blend! They are mixed together by shaking and stirring, or by adding another substance to mix things up. Some wallpaints are emulsions. They are made of small drops of color that are spread throughout another liquid, such as water.

WHICH FLAVOR?

You can guess a drink flavor by the color of the substances dissolved in the water. Orange drinks are orange flavored. Red drinks might be raspberry or cherry, and pale green is usually lime flavor.

IMAGINE THIS...

Wash your hands often to remove dirt and germs. Cold water alone is no good. Warm water and soap dissolve dirt properly and get your hands clean.

SIEVING

Sieves are used to separate mixtures. They have a mesh of little holes. Items smaller than the holes pass through, but bigger ones do not. Sieves are used to separate grains of wheat from the rest of the plant.

WHAT A MIX-UP!

Oh no! The salt has accidentally spilled into the sand. How can you separate this mixture of tiny grains? You could use a microscope and a very thin pair of tweezers, but that would take a very long time. Dissolving and **filtering** are much easier.

YOU WILL NEED:

- cupful of clean sand
- cupful of table salt
- pitcher and bowl
- funnel with filter paper, paper tissues, or paper towels
- warm water

1 Mix the grains of sand with the grains, or crystals, of salt. Put the mixture in a pitcher or bowl.

2 Add the warm water to dissolve the salt, stirring well until all of the salt crystals have disappeared.

3 Pour the pitcher's contents through some filter paper or a similar material in a funnel into a bowl.

4 Allow the funnel, paper, and sand to dry. Then you can brush off the sand.

Dissolving—the salt grains dissolve in water. They become smaller and smaller until they are the tiniest particles of salt, known as molecules. These are much too minute to see as they float among the water molecules.

5 Leave the salt solution to dry in a warm place. The water will evaporate, which means it will turn into a gaslike vapor that mixes invisibly in the air. The salt will be left, probably as a crust. Stir this to get back to salt crystals or grains.

Filtering—the filter is like a net with tiny holes. Molecules of water and salt are so small that they easily pass through the holes. But grains of sand are much too big to pass through.

FREEZING AND MELTING!

When water becomes very cold, a strange thing happens. It turns rock-hard! We say it **freezes** into ice. As the ice warms, the opposite happens. It turns back into a liquid—it **melts** into water. Other substances can be liquid and solid, too.

Solids are usually hard and keep their shape. Liquids move or flow and take up the shapes of their containers. If liquids are heated they turn into gases. These can also flow, and spread out to fill wherever they are. Whether a substance is solid, liquid, or gas is called its state.

ICICLES

In the cold of winter, dripping or falling water freezes into icicles. When the weather gets warmer, these melt back into a liquid state.

IMAGINE THIS...

Solid water, or ice, can be carved into amazing shapes. But it must stay frozen. Otherwise, the shape melts and drips away.

COLD

Air freezes   -362°F

Water freezes   32°F

16

HEAT AND MELTING

Metals and plastics are solid—but not always. It depends on how hot they are. If you heat plastic, it turns soft and runny and becomes a liquid. The same happens to metals, but they need much more heat, usually until they are red-hot.

RED-HOT

Hot liquid metal, such as this steel, is poured into a shape called a mold. After the metal cools and hardens, it keeps its shape.

Water boils	212°F		Gold melts	1,947°F		Iron melts	2,800°F	HOT

COLDER THAN ICE

How can water be colder than ice? Try adding some salt to it and see what happens.

2 Put both cups in the freezer. Look at them every five minutes. Which one freezes first? Does the salty water freeze at all?

1 Fill each cup about two-thirds with water. Stir as much salt as possible into one cup.

When you add salt to water, it dissolves and its tiny molecules spread among the water molecules. As the solution cools, the salt molecules stop the water molecules joining together to form ice.

SAFE ROADS

In icy conditions, a mixture of grit and salt is spread onto roads. Salt makes it hard for water on the road to freeze. The grit helps vehicles' tires grip.

POWER OF ICE

Have you heard how water pipes freeze in cold weather, then leak when they warm again, causing a flood? This is due to the power of ice.

YOU WILL NEED:
- plastic cup with lid
- plastic bowl
- water
- freezer

1 Completely fill the cup with water and put on the lid so that there is no air inside.

3 The water expands, or gets bigger, as it cools, and then freezes with enough power to push off the lid.

2 Put the cup in a plastic bowl (in case of spills) and put it in the freezer for a few hours.

Most substances expand as they get hotter. Water expands as it freezes and pushes out with such force that it can break a pipe or container.

PHEW, BOILING!

Adding heat to a substance can change it from a solid into a liquid. But what happens if things get even hotter?

More and more heat can cause various changes. Most substances get bigger, or expand, as they get hotter. When a liquid gets hot enough, it boils and turns into a gas, or a vapor. The vapor contains the same tiny pieces as the liquid but these are much farther apart, so we cannot see them. They spread out and float away in the air. If the vapor then cools, it turns back into its liquid form. This is known as condensation.

BOILING HOT

When liquid water is heated enough, it turns into a gas called water vapor, or steam. Steam is useful for cleaning fabrics and is helpful in ironing creases out of clothes.

IMAGINE THIS...

Steam can also be used to make power. Hot rocks deep underground heat water, and this steamy water can be used to make electricity— and a nice, hot bath.

Lead boils 3,180°F

Mercury boils 674.4°F

Olive oil boils 572°F)

Water boils 212°F

Ammonia boils -31.9°F

Hydrogen boils -423°F

BOILING POINT

The temperature at which a liquid turns into a gas is called its boiling point. Some substances, such as hydrogen, have a very low boiling point. Others, such as metals, have boiling points that are thousands of degrees.

COOL STUFF

When a gas cools enough, it turns back into a liquid. You can see this when steam touches a cool window and condenses back into liquid water.

SUBLIME STUFF

Some substances can change from a solid straight into a gas, without being a liquid. This is called **sublimation**. Dry ice is the solid form of carbon dioxide. It must be kept very cold. If it gets above -29.9°F it turns into a gas.

CARRY OR NOT?

Leave a metal teaspoon in a hot drink and gradually it gets warm. Yet a plastic teaspoon in the same drink does not become warm. Heat passes through certain substances and materials, but not others.

Substances that are good at carrying heat are known as thermal conductors. They include most metals. This is why wood burners, coal stoves, and central heating radiators are made of metal. They conduct the heat from inside to warm the air. Metal pans conduct heat from the flame or stove below to the food inside.

Substances that are bad at carrying heat are called thermal insulators. They include wood, cardstock, plastic, pottery, and textiles. Many pans have plastic handles, which do not carry heat from the pan to the part that people touch.

KEEPING OUT HEAT

Pots and pans get much too hot to touch. Oven gloves are made of fabrics and padding that are good thermal insulators. They allow heat to pass through only very slowly.

KEEP IN THE HEAT

The home you live in is made from substances that are good at conducting heat. This picture shows how much heat is lost through different parts of a house. Keeping the roof and walls insulated and blocking drafts should keep you feeling cozy and your fuel bills low.

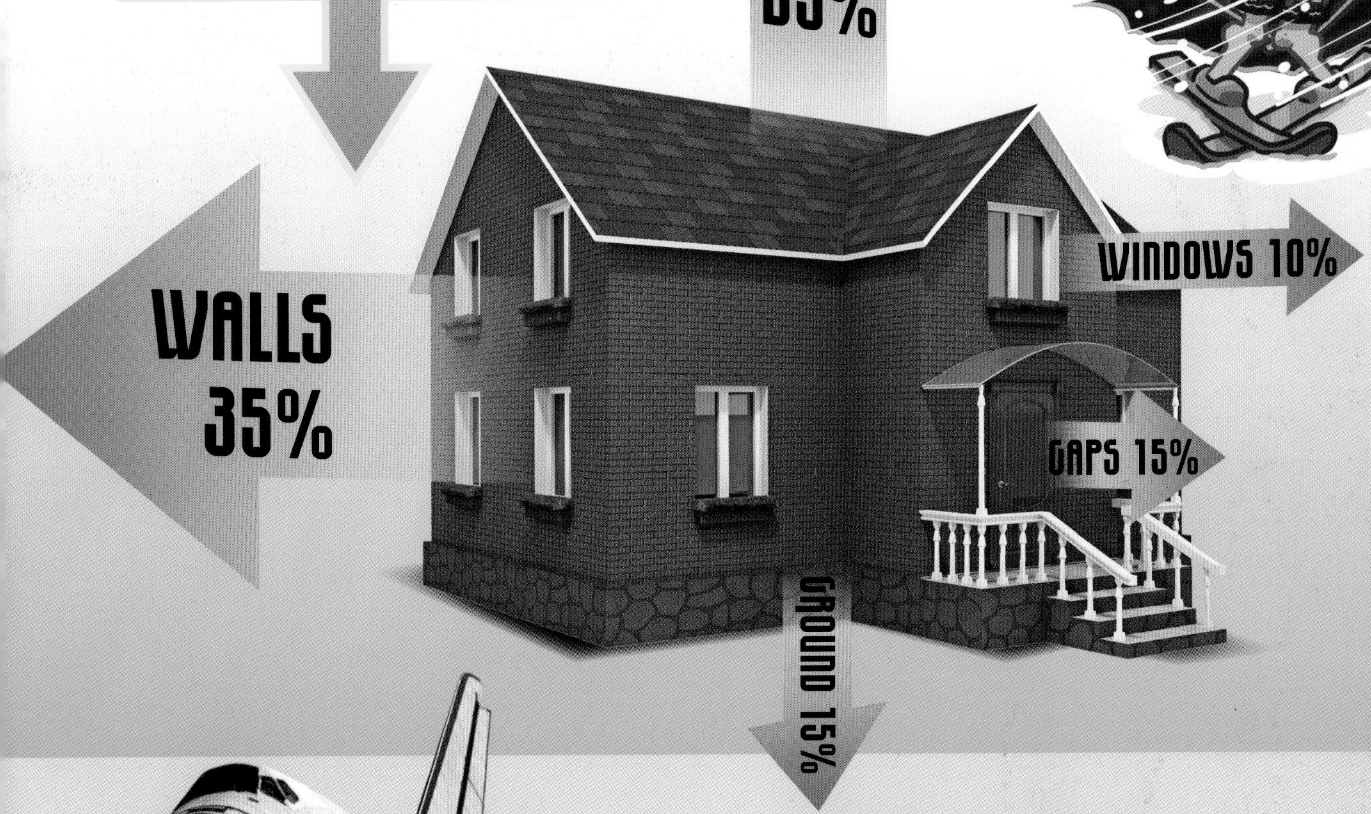

IMAGINE THIS...

Wearing the right clothes on a cold day will keep you warm—you wouldn't go skiing in just your bathing suit!

ROOF 25%

WALLS 35%

WINDOWS 10%

GAPS 15%

GROUND 15%

HEAT SHIELD

When spacecraft return to Earth, they become very hot as they enter the atmosphere. To stop them from burning up, they are covered in special substances that do not conduct heat. The bottom of the space shuttle has thick tiles that create a heat shield.

Space shuttle

CARRY THAT HEAT!

Which substances are good heat carriers, or conductors? Metals are good conductors, as this tasty test shows.

YOU WILL NEED:

- small lump of butter
- frozen peas
- long items such as metal spoon, metal kebab skewer, drinking straw, wooden or plastic chopstick, knitting needle
- pitcher of warm (not boiling) water
- adult help

2 Ask an adult to pour the warm water into the pitcher, then watch and wait.

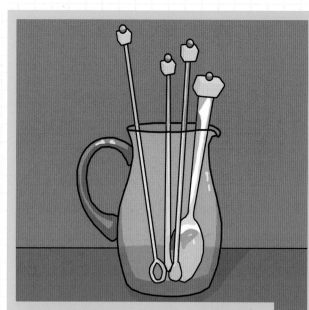

1 Put the long items in the pitcher. Stick a pea to the top of each item with a small lump of butter.

3 Which pea falls off first? The item it is stuck to is the best heat conductor. It carries heat from the water up to melt the butter. Which is the worst conductor or the best insulator?

You could try this test using chocolate instead of butter. Chocolate needs more heat to melt, but it's tastier!

STOP THAT HEAT!

Which substances are good insulators and the worst conductors? Sometimes we want to stop heat moving around.

YOU WILL NEED:

- two plastic cups
- two ice cubes
- various materials such as cotton handkerchief, aluminum foil, bubble wrap, plastic wrap, paper towel
- thermos

2 Wrap up the cups in the various materials. Leave one of the cups unwrapped.

3 Every few minutes, check the cups and flask to see which ice cubes are melting and which are still frozen. Then wrap them again.

1 Put an ice cube in each plastic cup and one in the thermos.

The materials around the cubes that stay frozen the longest are the best insulators. Does the cube in the thermos last the longest?

25

DON'T TOUCH!

"Danger! If this chemical touches the skin, wash it off at once with plenty of clean water, and seek medical advice!" Substances such as powerful chemicals need these health warnings.

Chemicals such as bleaches, oven cleaners, rust removers, insect killers, and drain clearers must be powerful in order to do their job. They cause chemical changes or reactions such as clearing blockages and dissolving dirt and grease. Some chemicals are strong acids, such as the hydrochloric acid in a car battery. They can damage substances by eating away at them. Other **corrosive** chemicals are alkalies, such as drain clearer. All of these powerful chemicals must be handled with care!

Chemical Labels

Dangerous chemicals usually have warning labels on them to tell people they're dangerous. Never put chemicals, liquids, powders, or similar substances into other containers, especially if they have the wrong label or no label at all.

26

IN THE FACTORY

Factory workers who use powerful chemicals are trained to understand the dangers, know about safety, and wear protective equipment. They should know what to do in case a chemical splashes or spills.

PESTICIDES

Pesticides kill damaging small creatures, such as caterpillars, worms, slugs, and grubs. But they may also harm people and pets. Farmers need to read the instructions and follow them carefully.

OUT OF REACH

In the home, powerful chemicals must be kept out of reach of young children who do not understand the dangers. In a locked cupboard or on a high shelf is a good place.

KITCHEN CHEMISTRY

School lessons teach us about different materials, heat and cold, freezing, melting and boiling, mixtures, and changes. But what can you learn at home?

The kitchen is a great place to learn about chemical changes and physical processes. Soaps are used to dissolve dirt and grease off hands, dishes, and work surfaces. Ingredients are mixed in all sorts of combinations and can be heated in an oven or on a stove. Refrigerators and freezers keep food cold and help them stay fresher for longer.

CHANGING FOOD

By mixing different foods together, cooks can change what they look like, how they taste, and even how they behave. Jello is made by adding hot water to jello powder, pouring the runny liquid into a shape or mold, and then allowing it to cool. In hot weather, keep jello in the refrigerator or it will start to melt again.

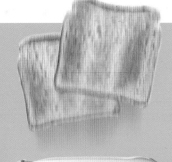

ADDING HEAT

Heating foods can change them and make them good to eat. Boiling potatoes in water makes them soft, while broiling pieces of meat makes them tender and delicious. A kitchen may have several different ways of heating food. These include microwave and normal ovens, and stoves that have gas or electric burners to heat pans. Toasters have electric heating elements to warm bread to make toast.

KEEP IT COOL

Refrigerators keep food and drinks cool. This slows down the rate at which food goes bad and keeps it fresh for several days. Freezers are even colder. They can freeze liquids solid and stop food from going bad for weeks and even months.

IMAGINE THIS...

Refrigerators and freezers allow us to safely store and keep large amounts of food. Without them, we would have to eat all our food very quickly—or go shopping a lot.

ERUPTION!

Some chemicals react together to make new substances that are gases. You can see how this happens with a homemade erupting volcano!

YOU WILL NEED:

- tray
- plastic cup
- vinegar
- red food coloring
- baking soda
- sand or papier mâché

2 Make a volcano around the cup by building up sand or papier mâché in a cone shape.

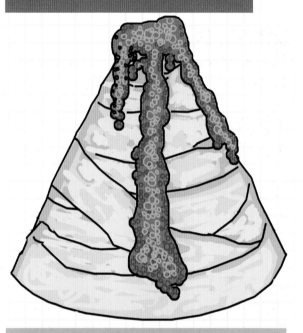

3 Add some of the baking soda into the vinegar, and watch what happens. The volcano bubbles and foams, just like a real one!

1 Put the cup on the tray. Fill the cup with vinegar. Add red food coloring for effect.

Vinegar contains the chemical acetic acid, and baking soda is sodium bicarbonate. When they mix, they cause a reaction that gives off the gas carbon dioxide, which makes the volcano "erupt."

GLOSSARY

ARTIFICIAL
Something that has been made by humans and does not occur naturally.

BOIL
When something warms up so much that it turns from a liquid into a gas.

BOILING POINT
The temperature at which something turns from a liquid into a gas.

BRITTLE
Something that will break very easily.

CORROSIVE
A chemical that slowly destroys something else.

DISSOLVING
Breaking up into such small pieces that the pieces from one substance mix completely with another substance.

FILTERING
Separating two substances by passing them through a sieve.

FLEXIBLE
Something that will bend without breaking.

FREEZE
When something cools so much that it turns from a liquid into a solid.

MELT
When something warms up so much that it turns from a solid into a liquid.

RAW MATERIALS
Natural substances that can be used to make artificial chemicals and substances.

RECYCLE
To reuse something, either in the same state or changed to make something new.

RIGID
Something that will not bend.

SOLUTE
A substance that dissolves into another.

SOLVENT
A substance, usually a liquid, that other substances dissolve into.

SUBLIMATION
When something warms up and turns straight from a solid into a gas, without becoming a liquid in between.

INDEX

FURTHER INFORMATION

www.eia.doe.gov/kids/energy.
cfm?page=sf_experiments
Lots of fun science fair experiments

http://yucky.discovery.com/flash/
fun_n_games/
Experiment with this fun kitchen
chemistry web site